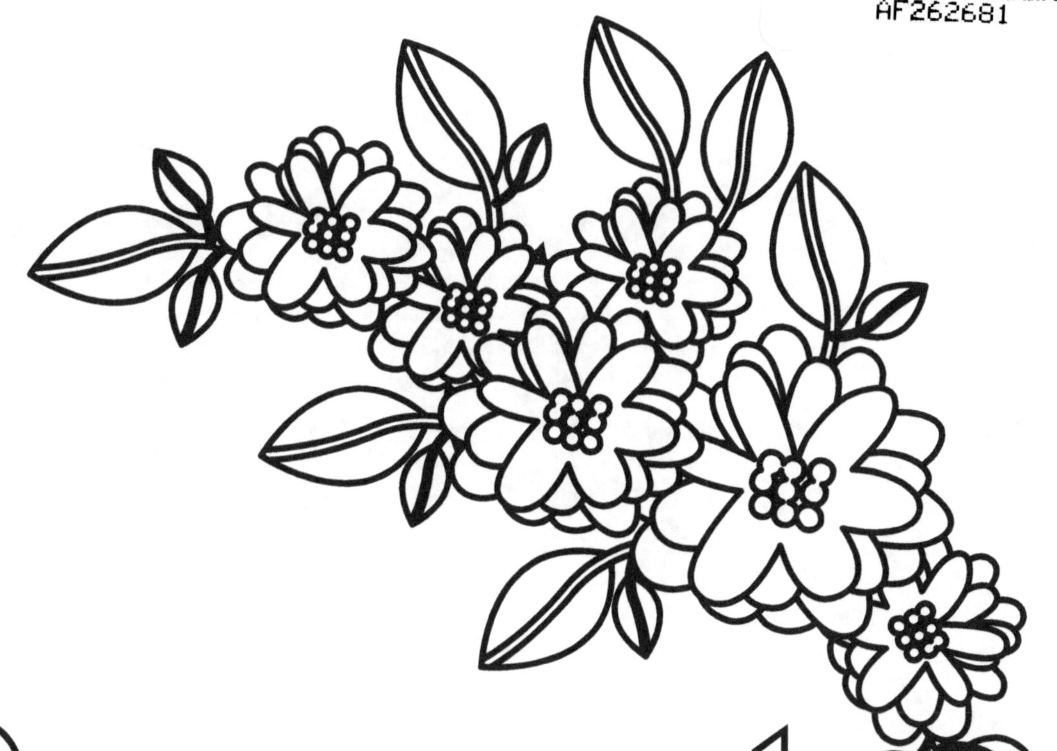

Pregnant with twins

by Naomi Dorland

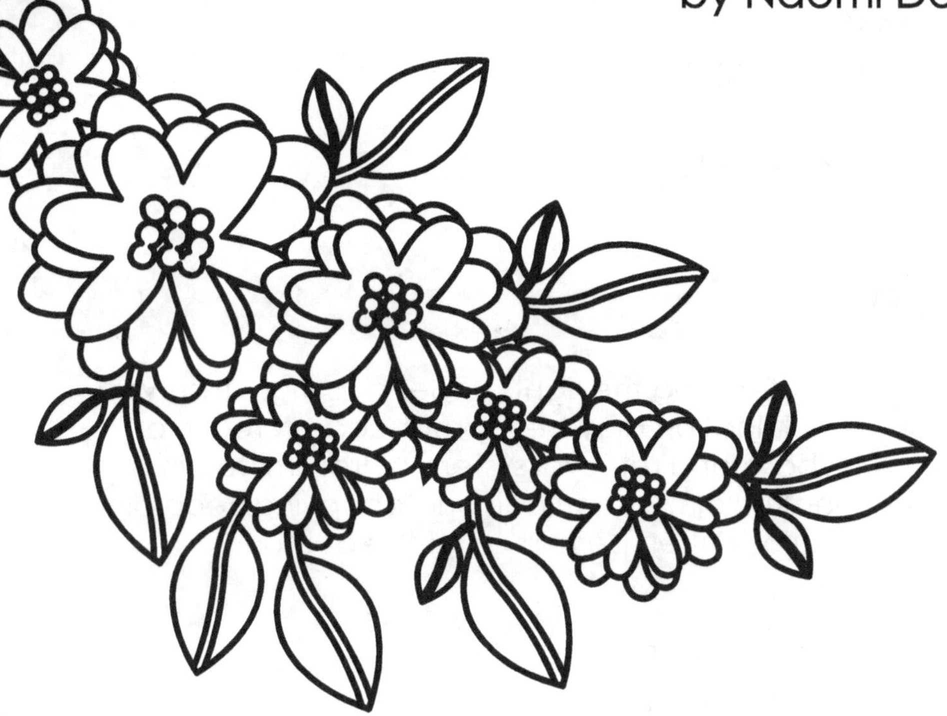

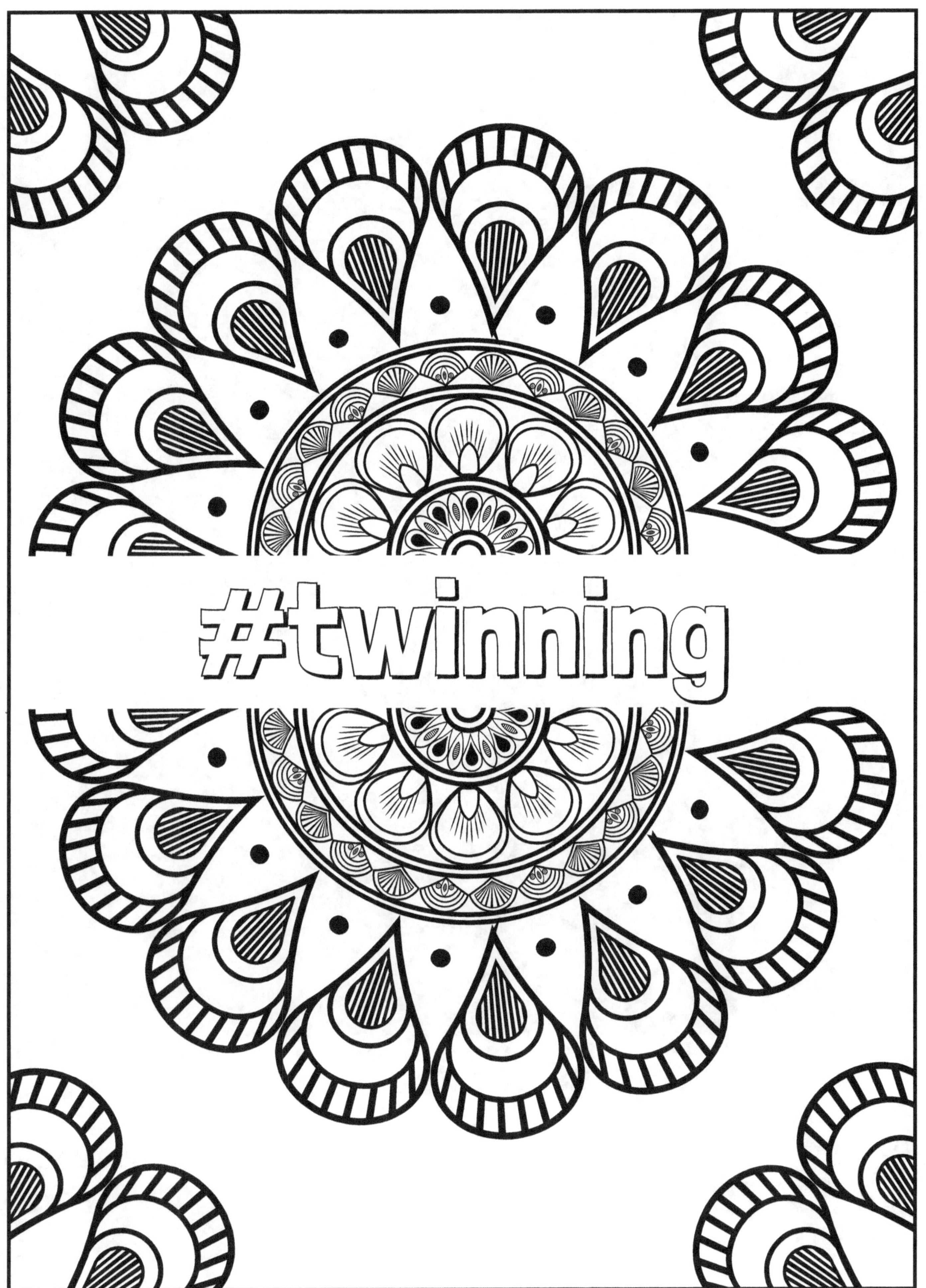
#twinning

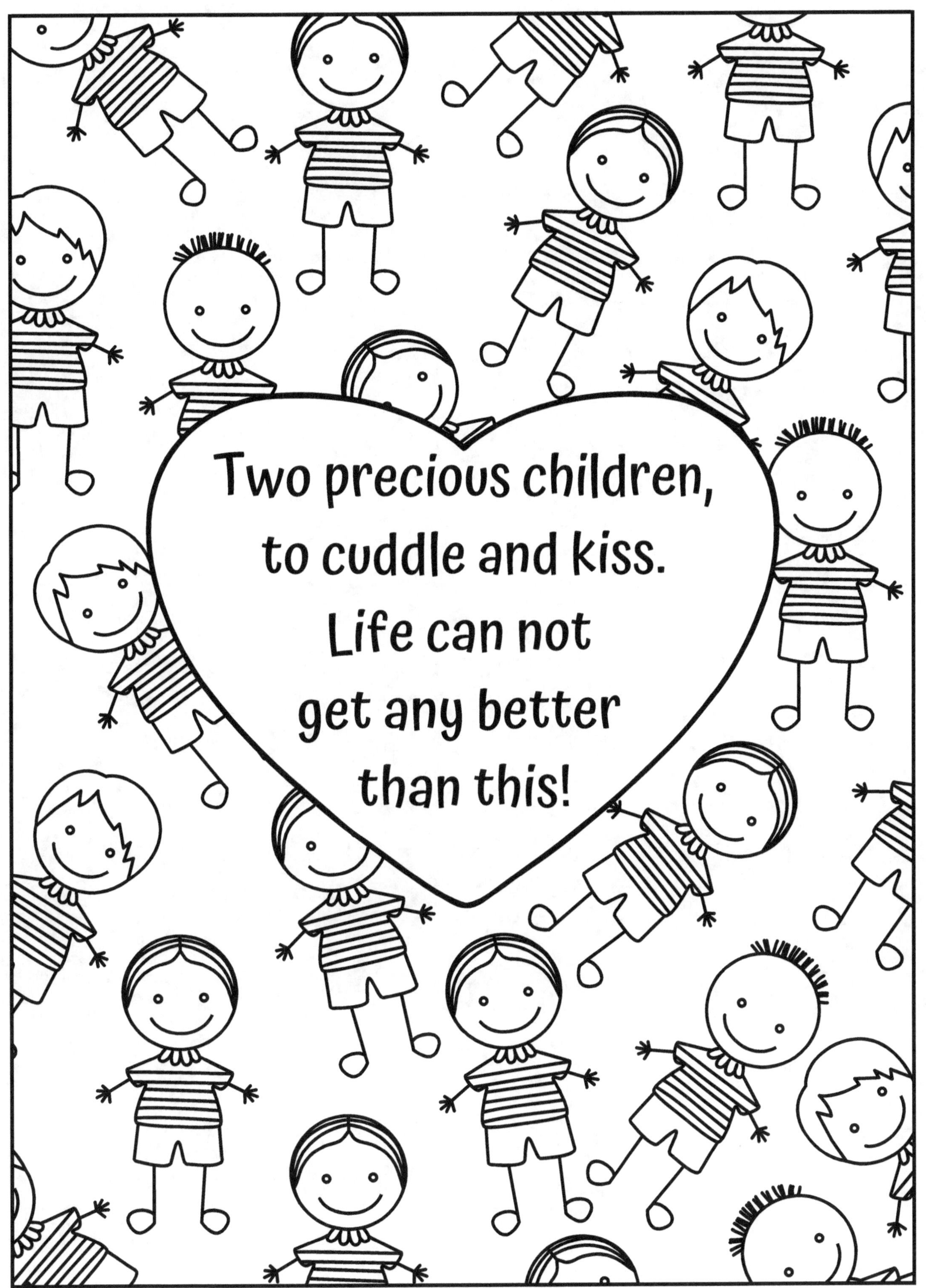

Two precious children,
to cuddle and kiss.
Life can not
get any better
than this!

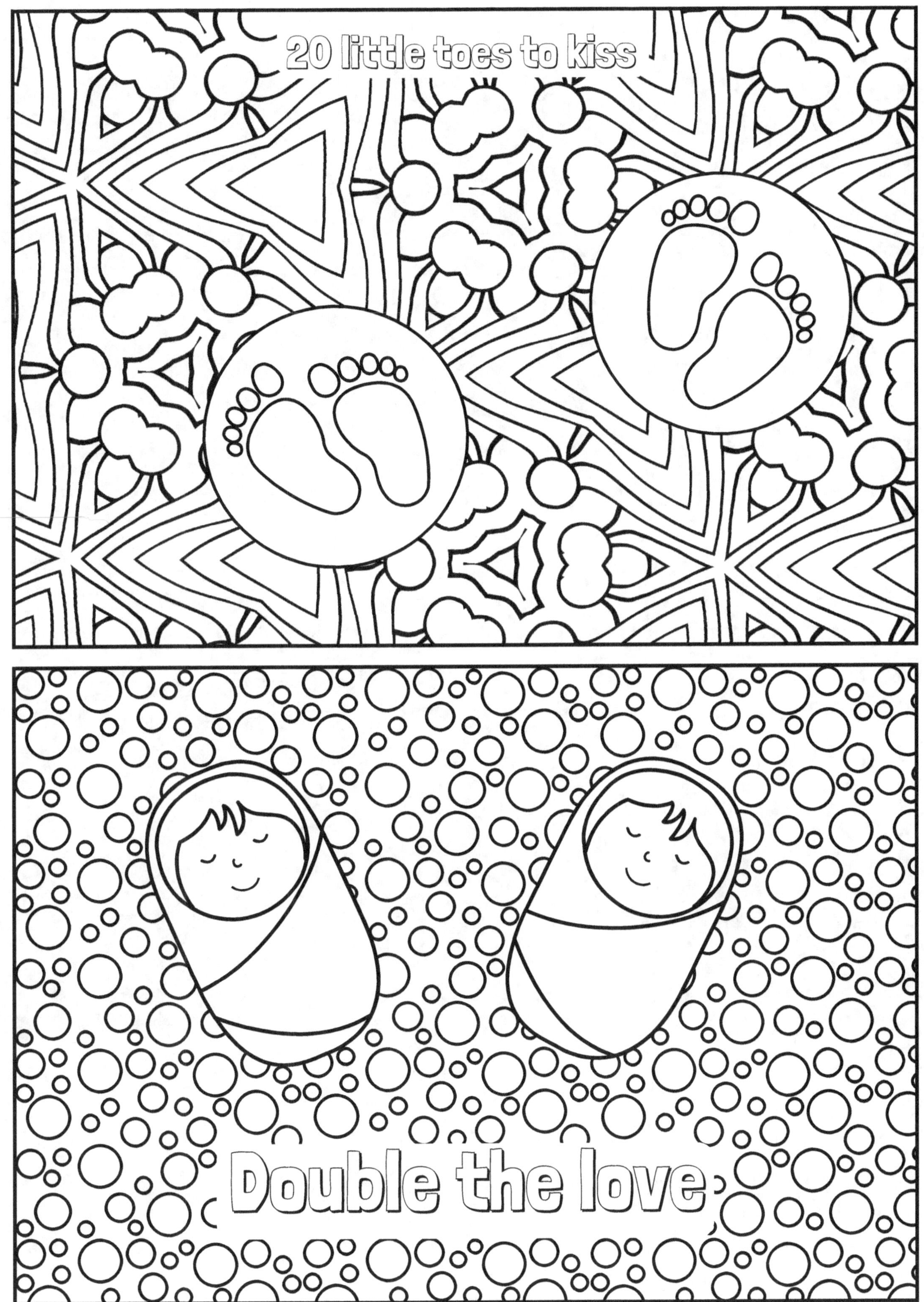

20 little toes to kiss
Double the love

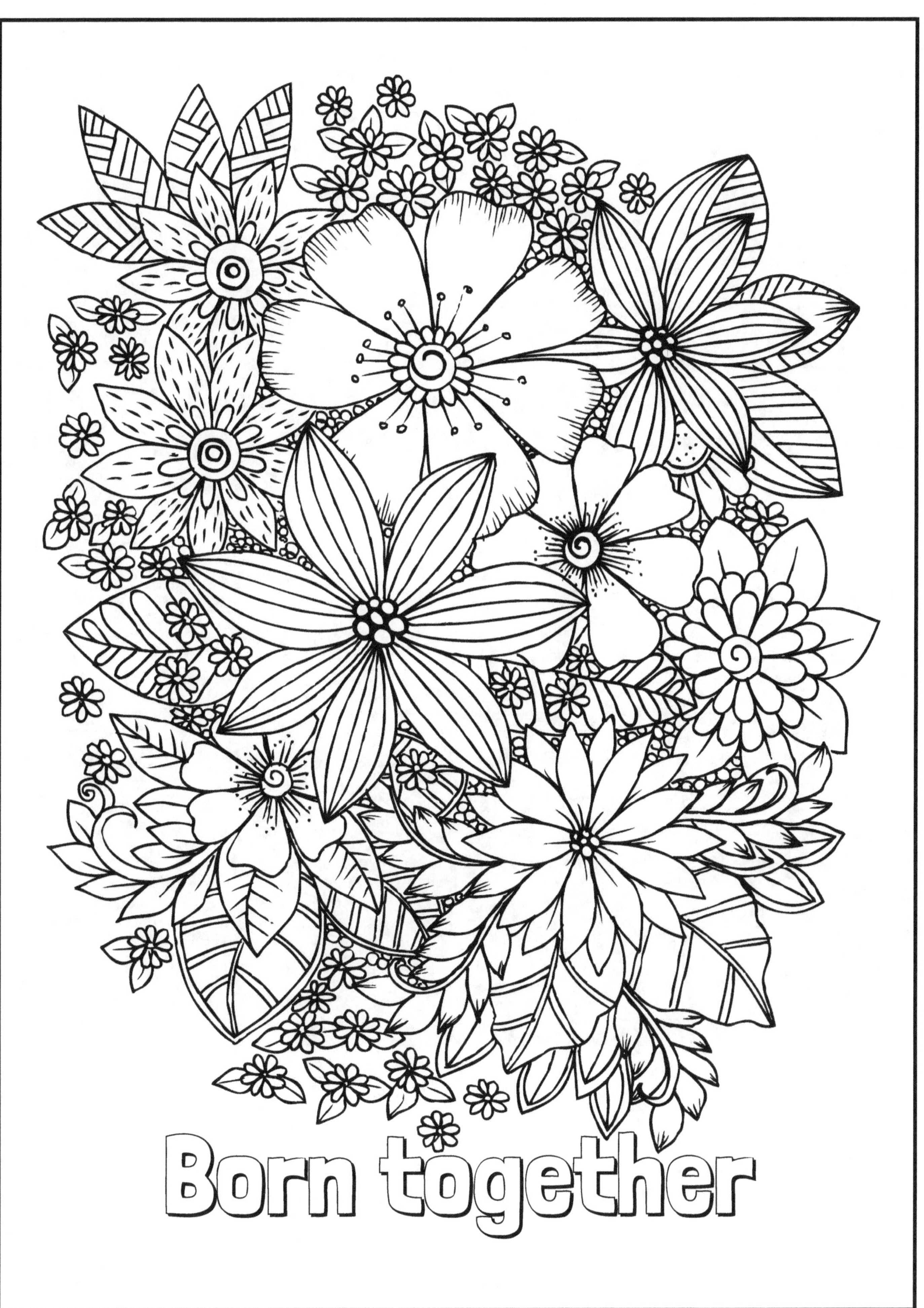

Born together

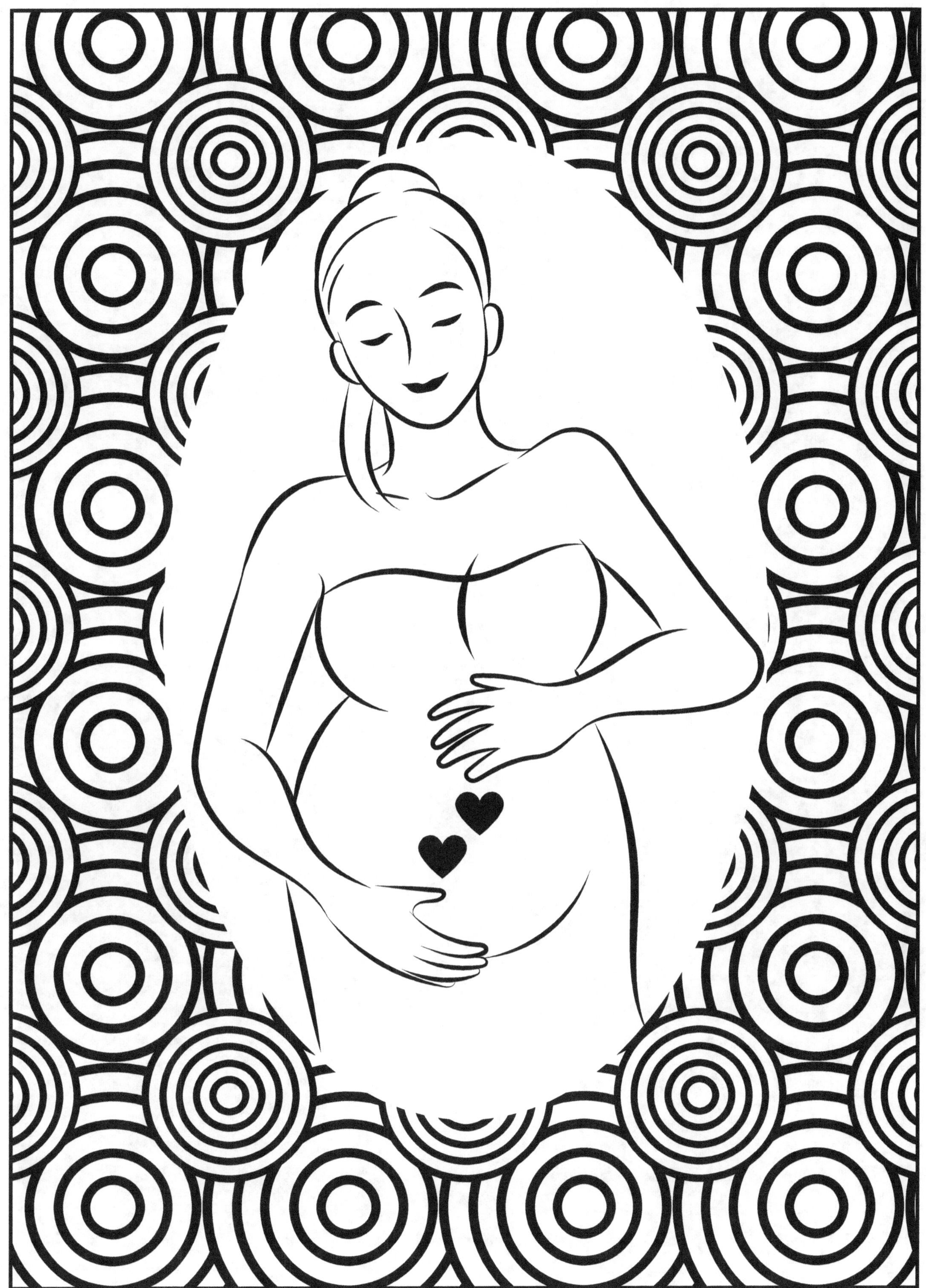

Double
blessings

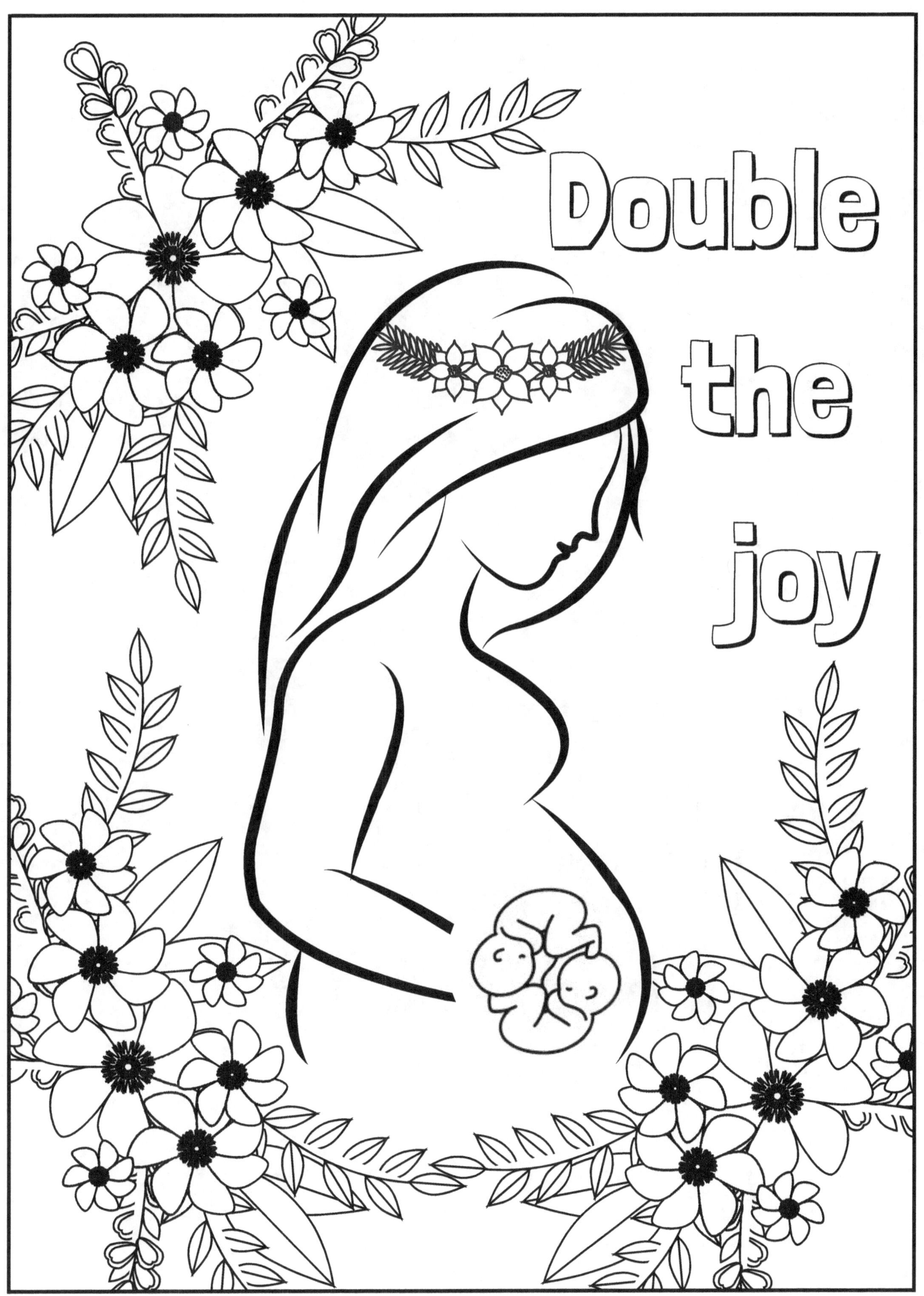

Double
the
joy

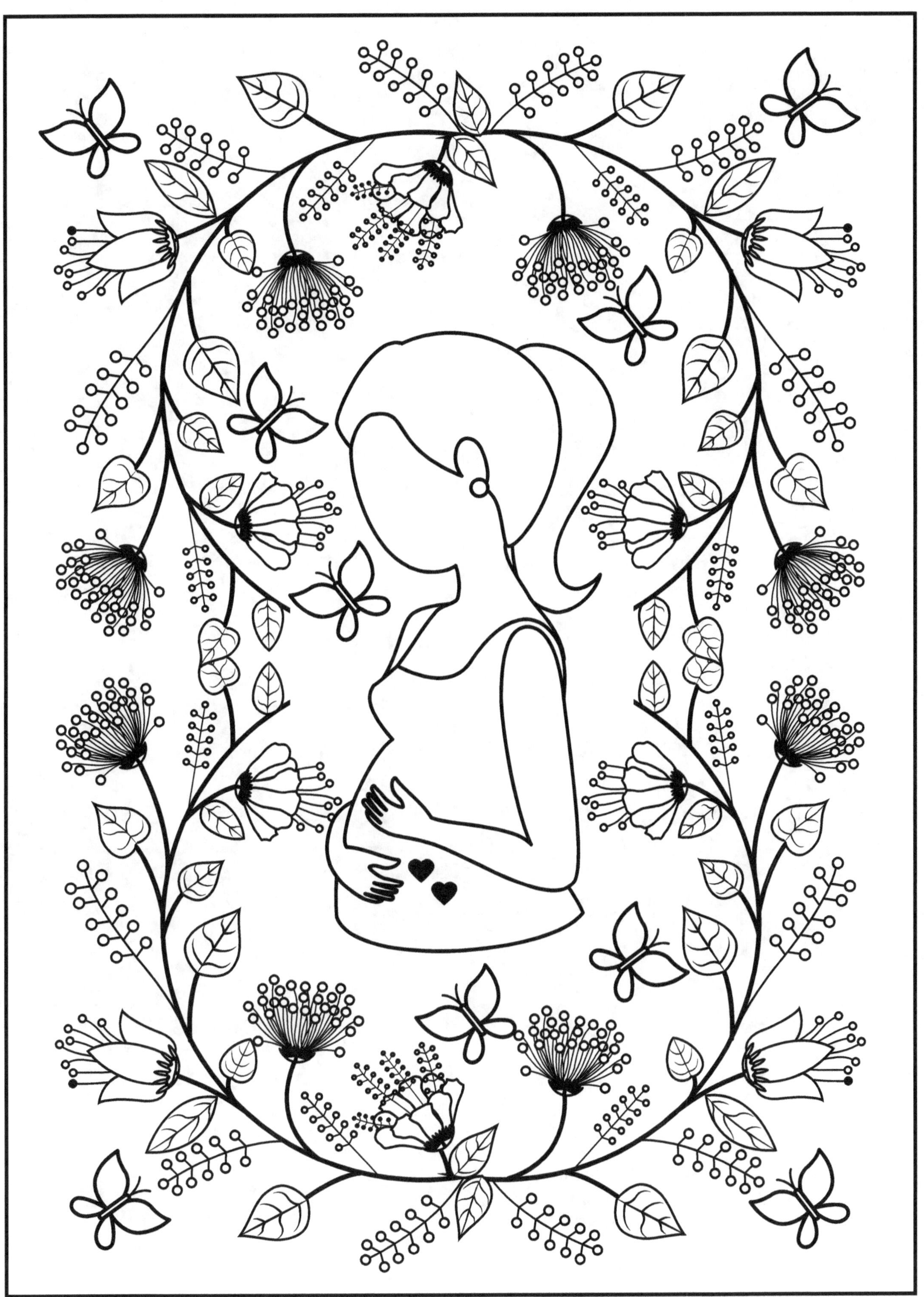

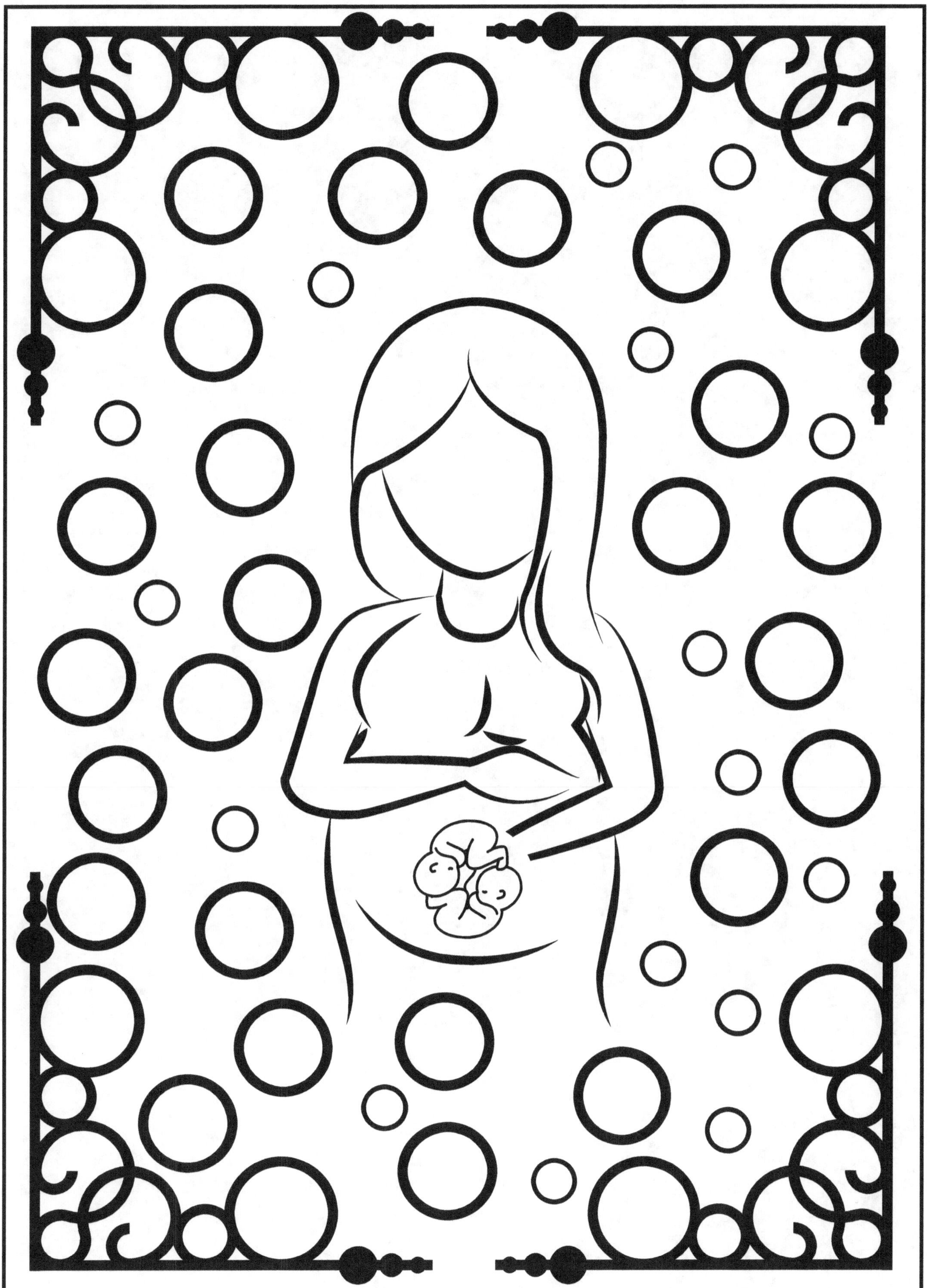

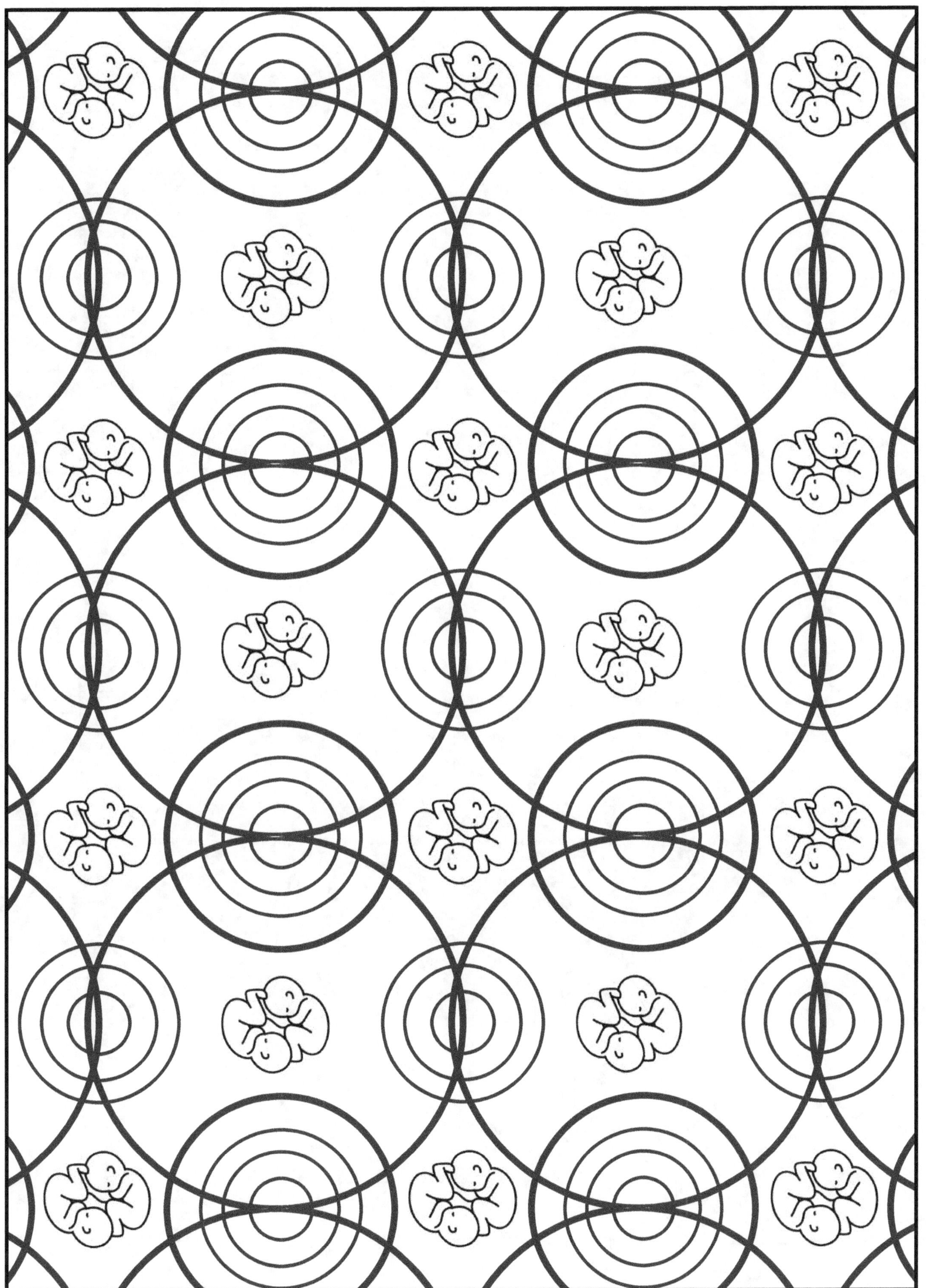

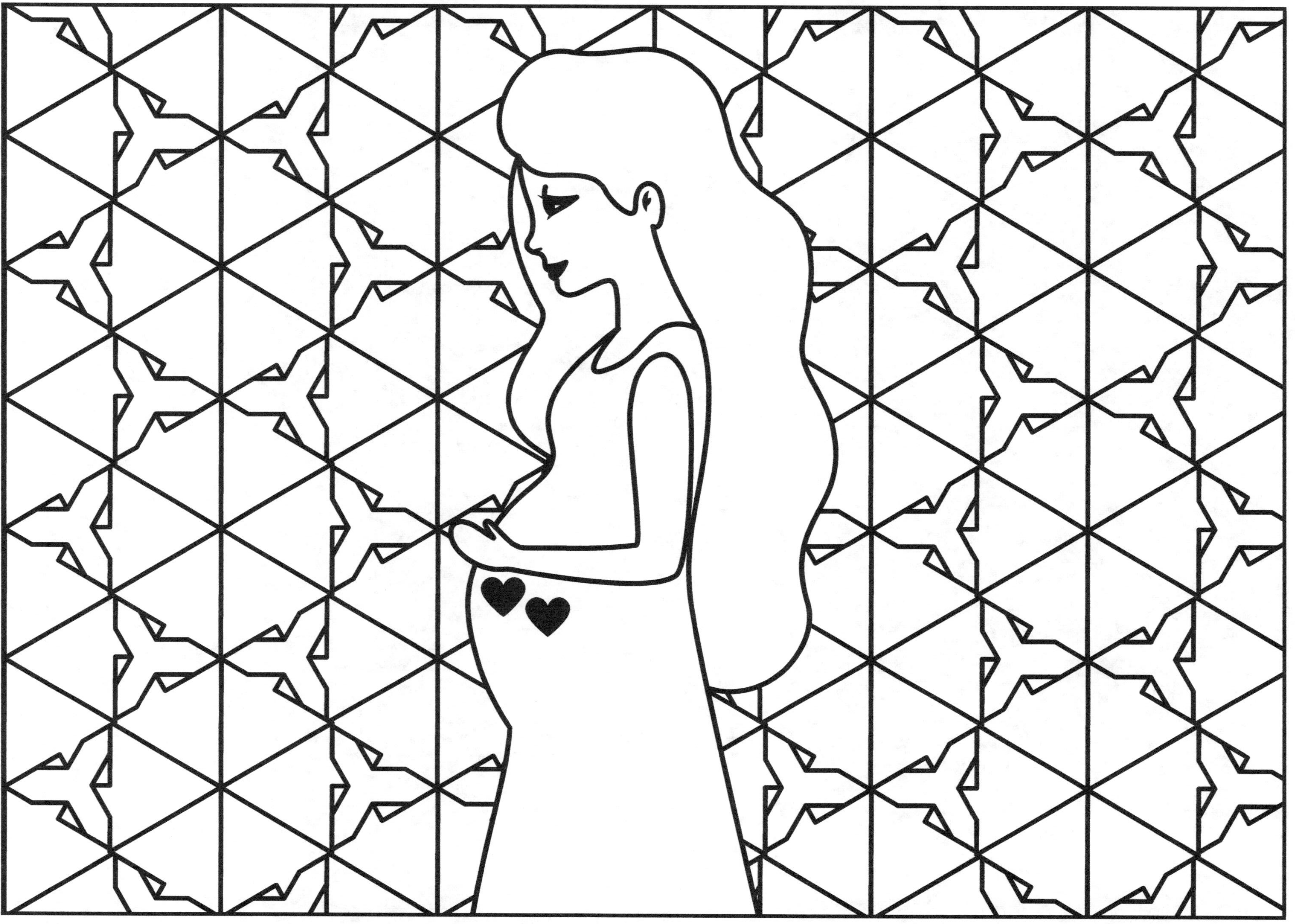

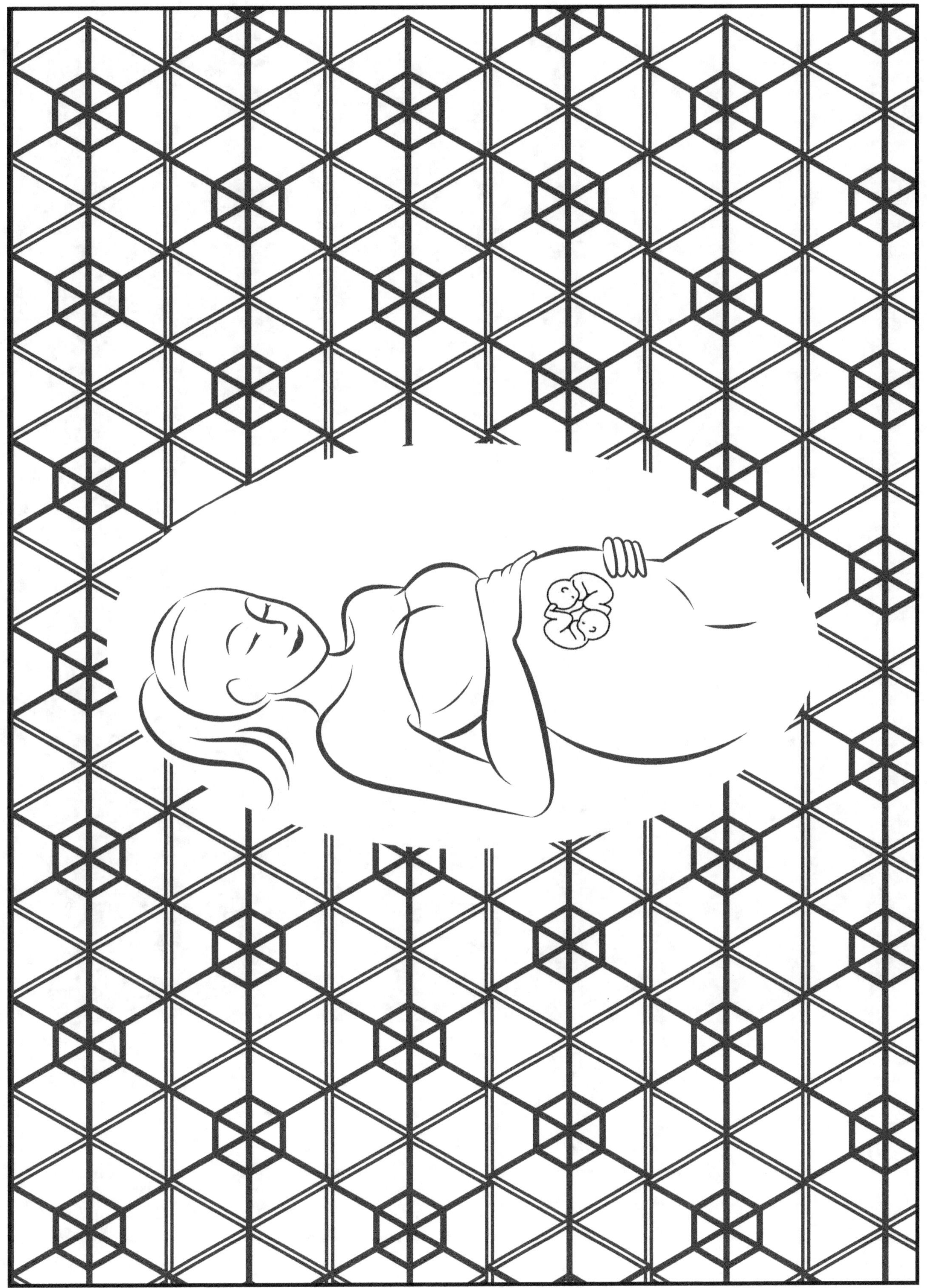

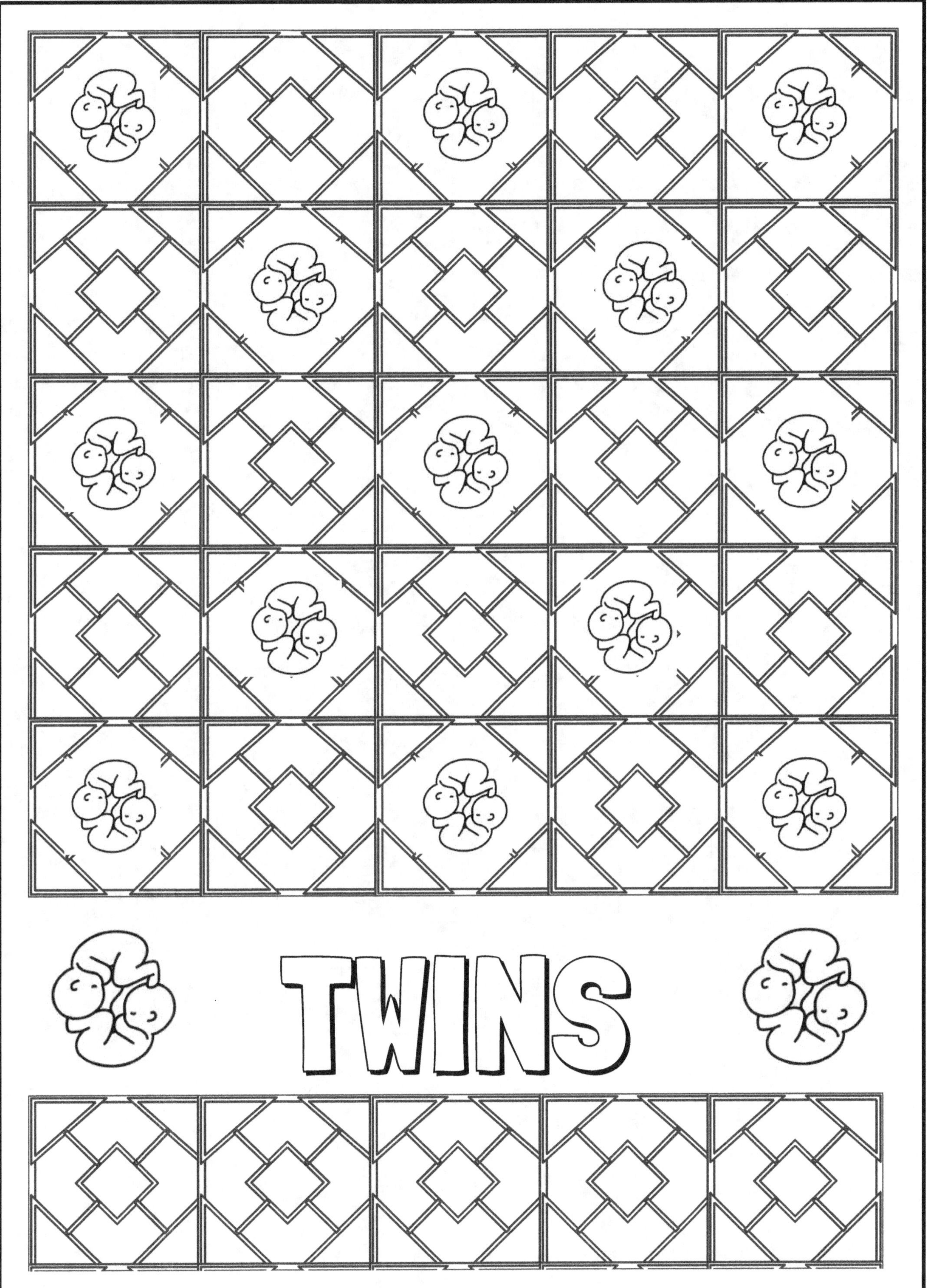
TWINS

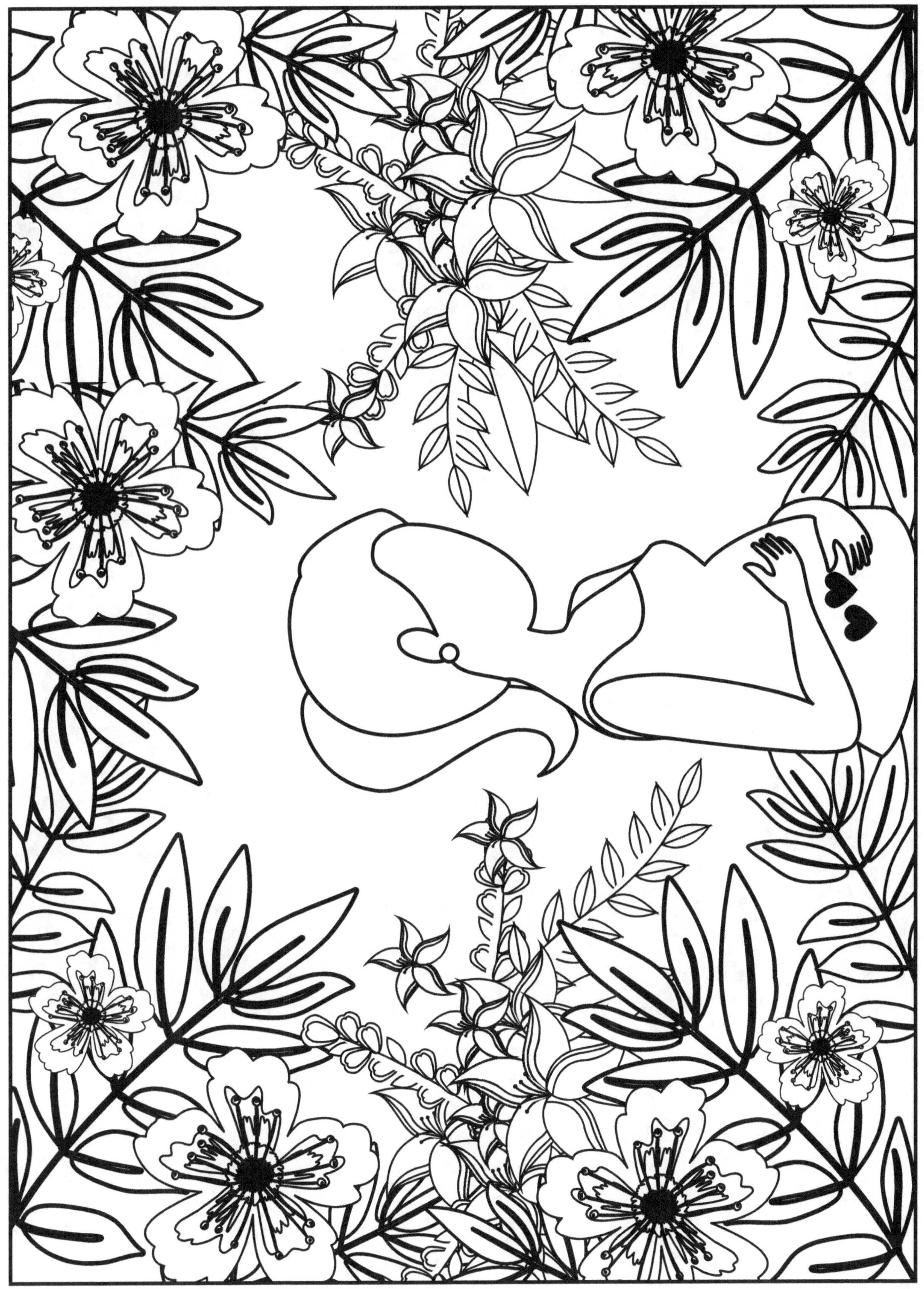

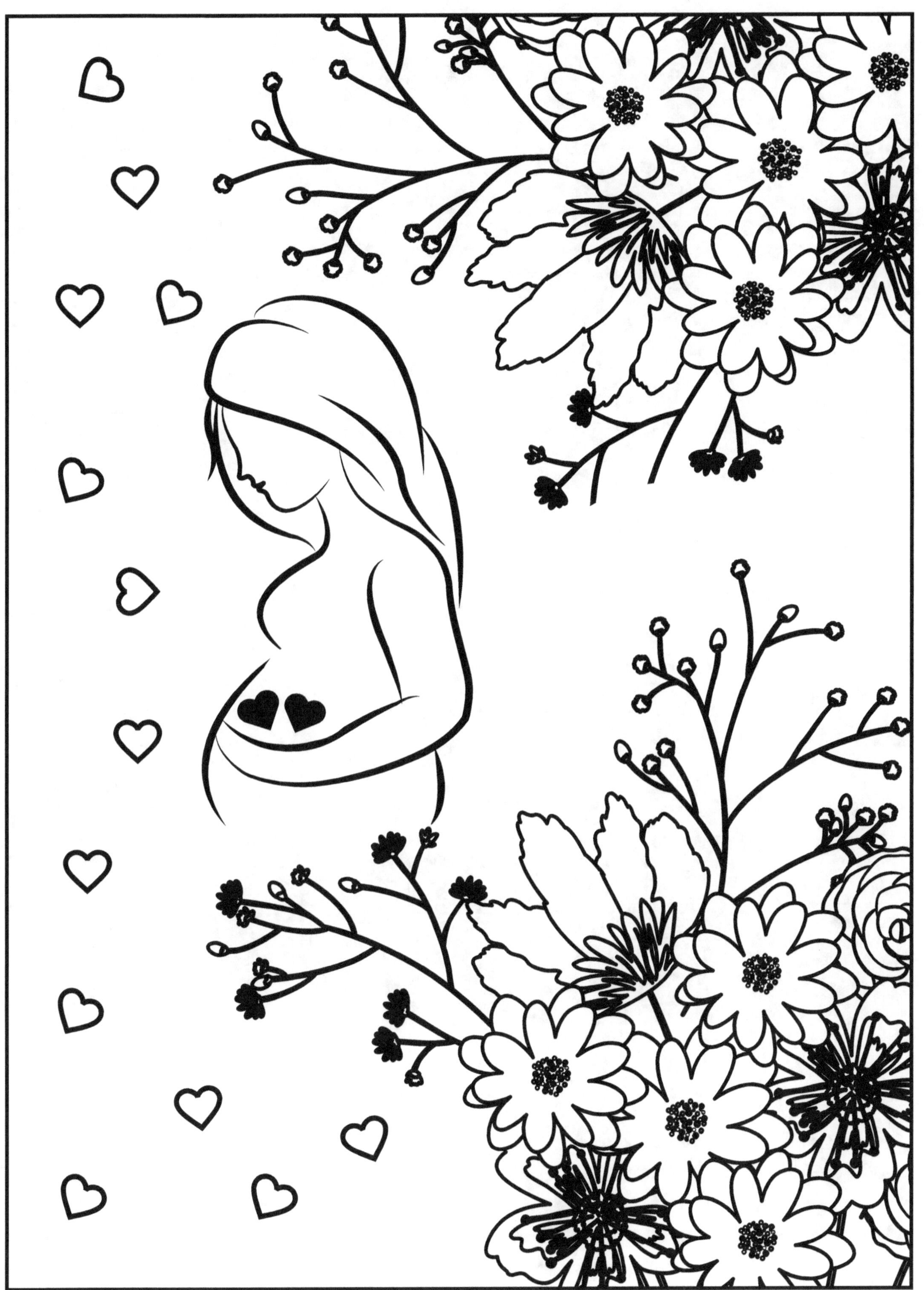

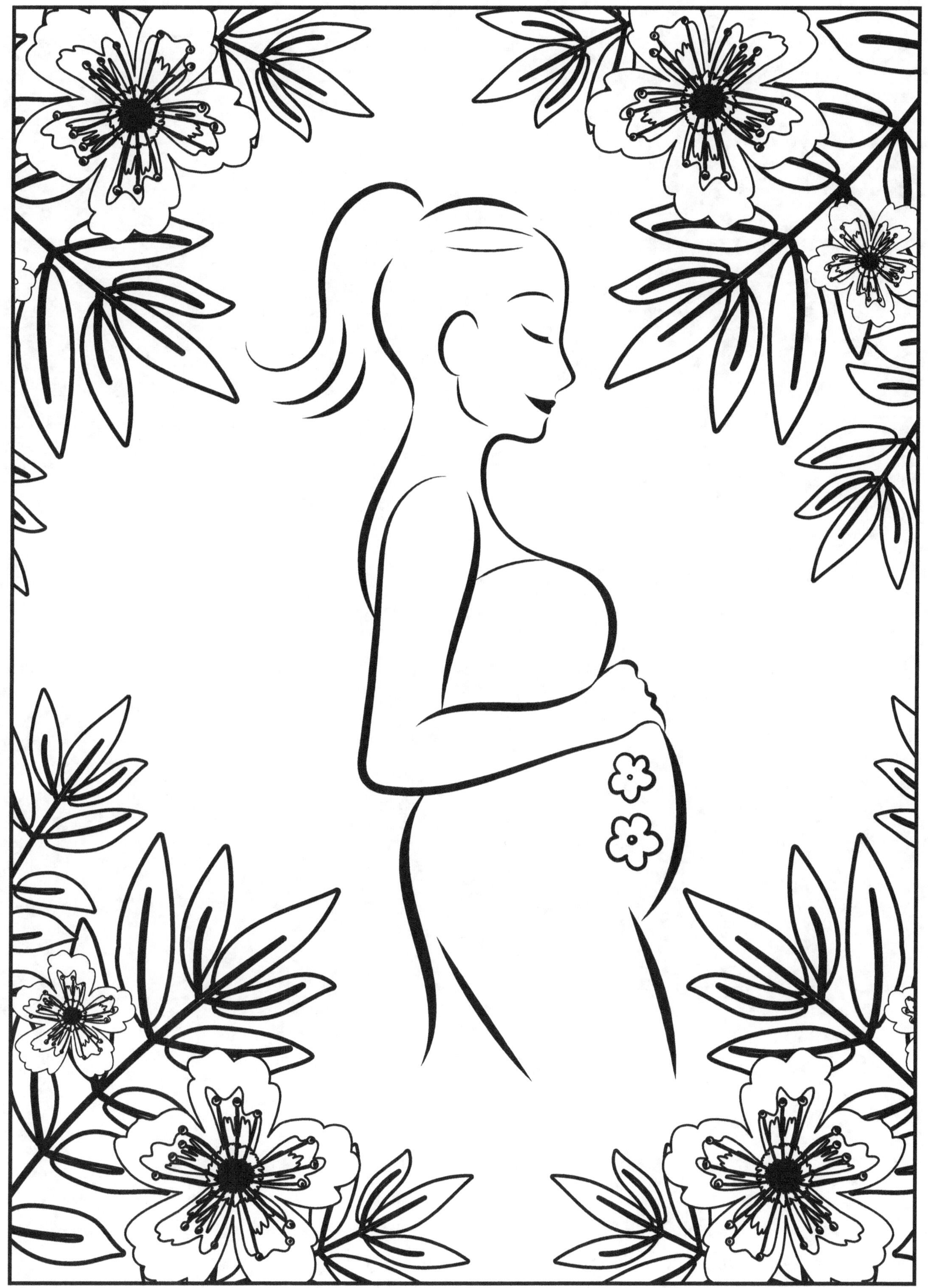

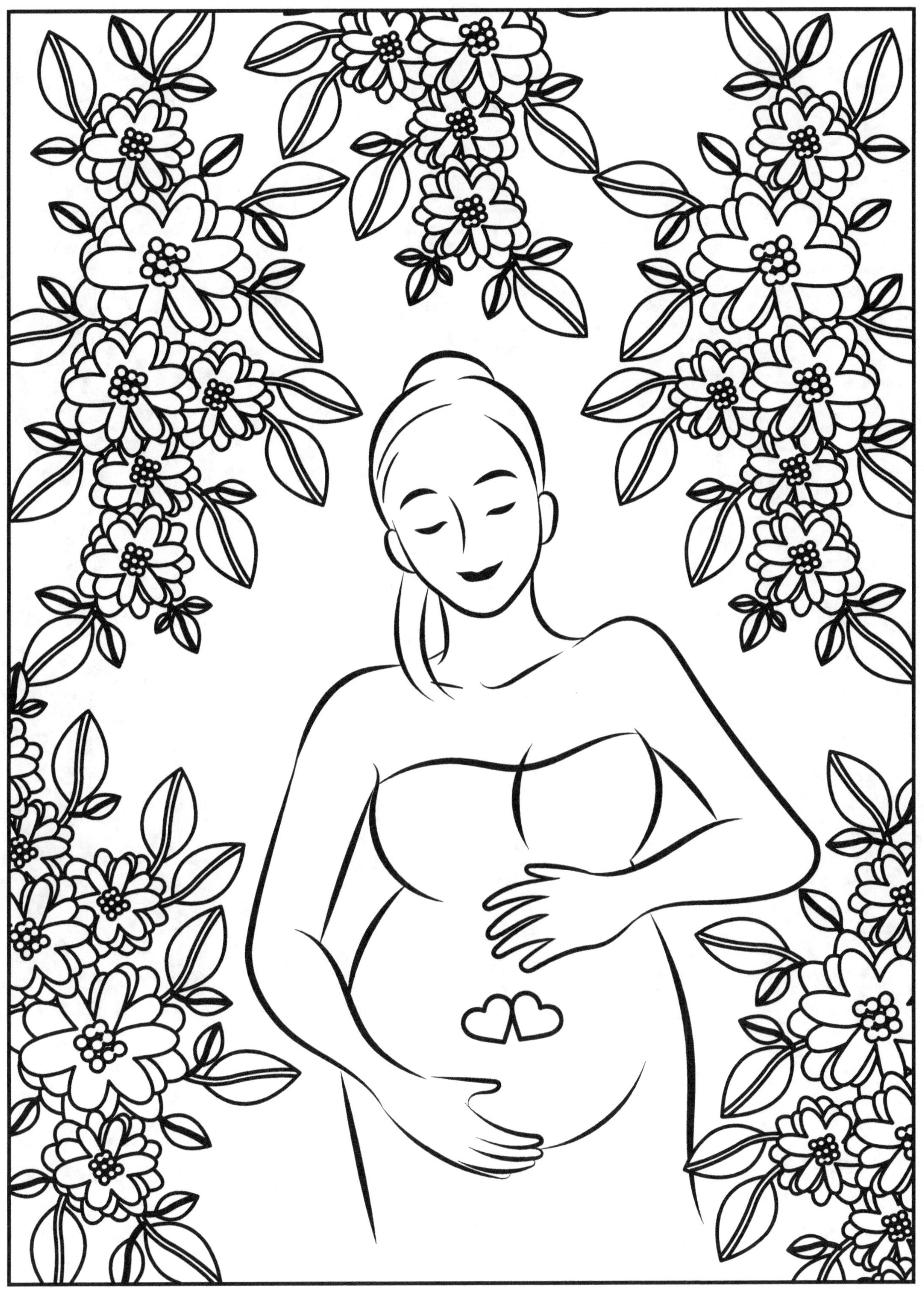

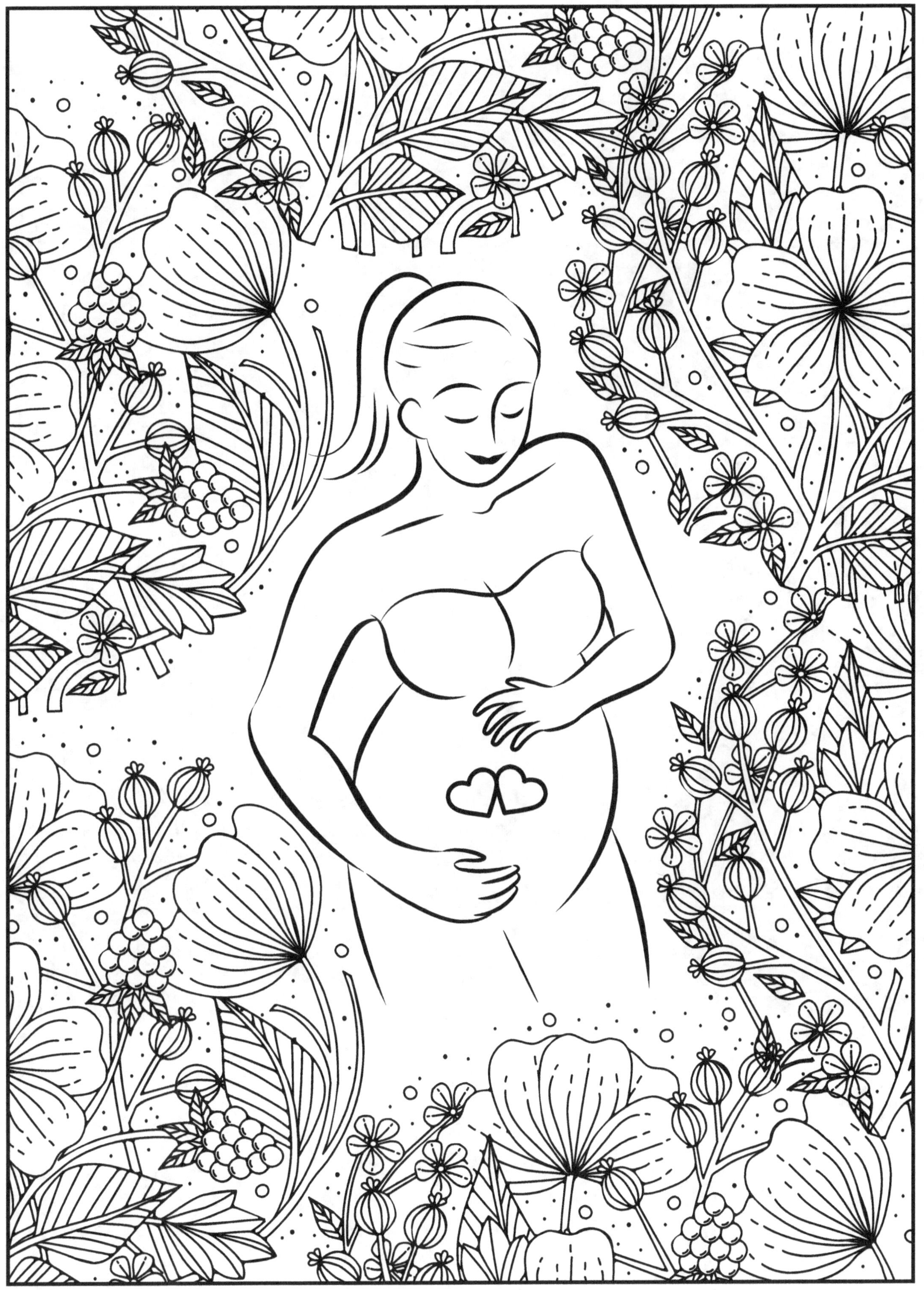

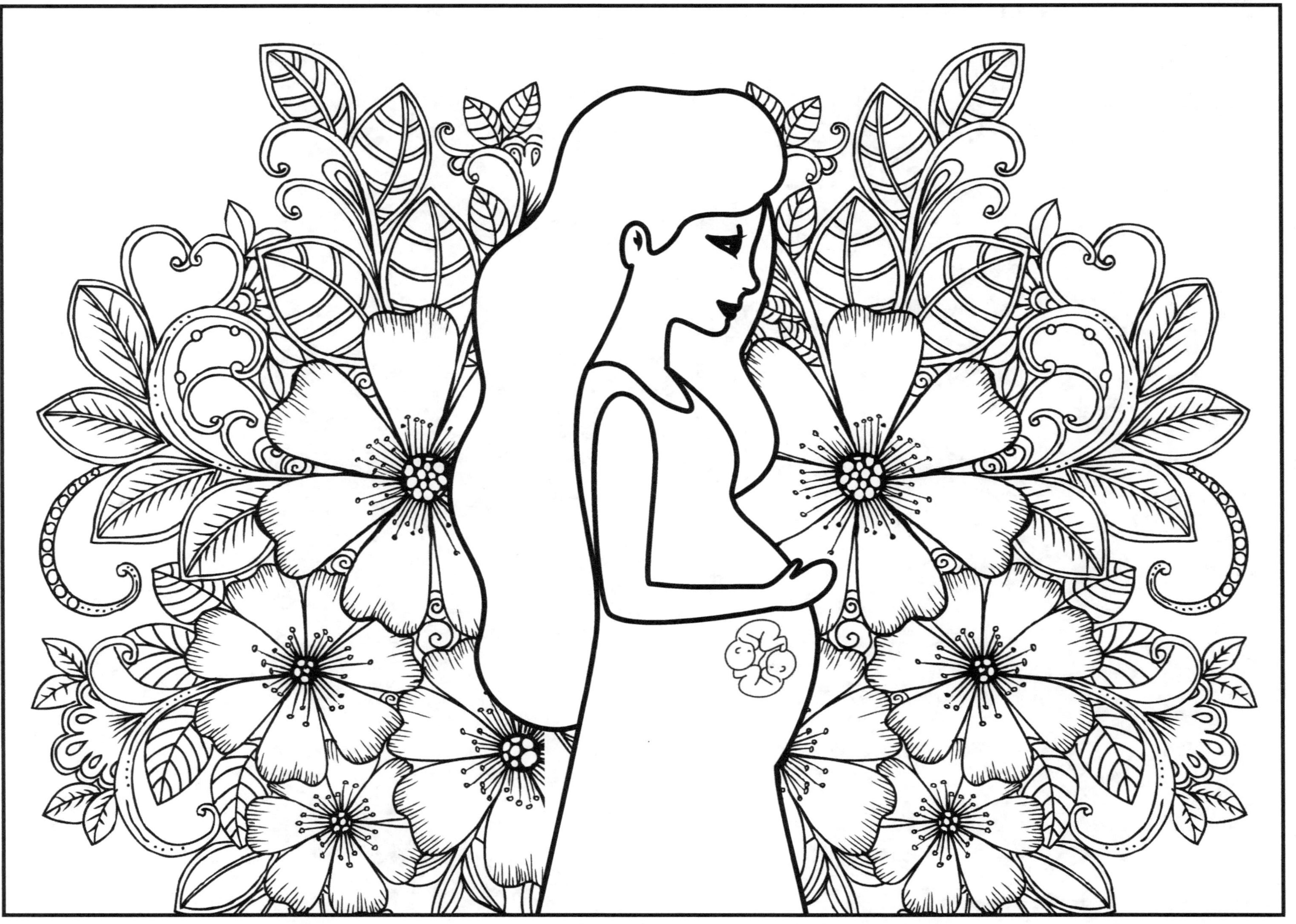

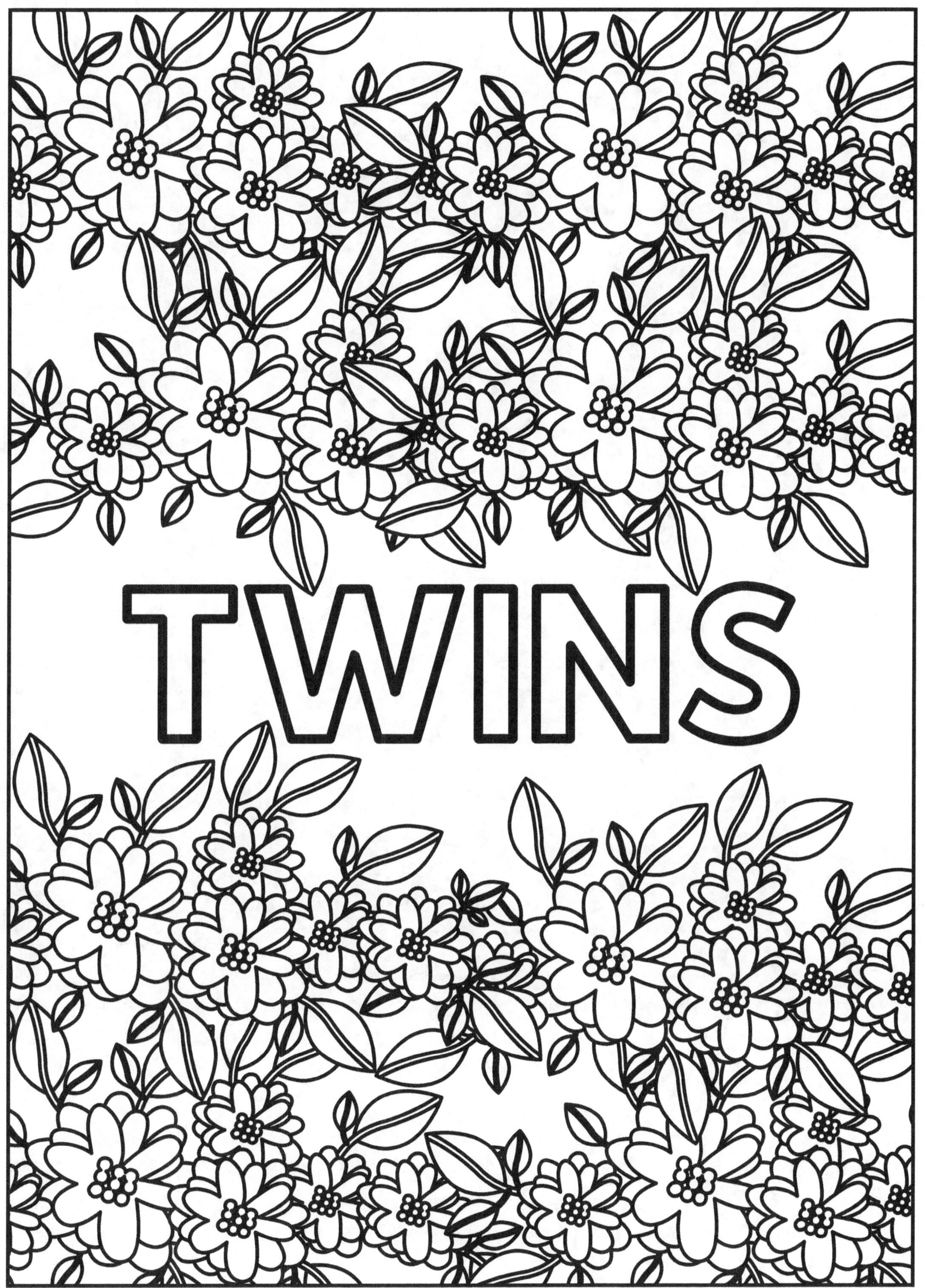
TWINS

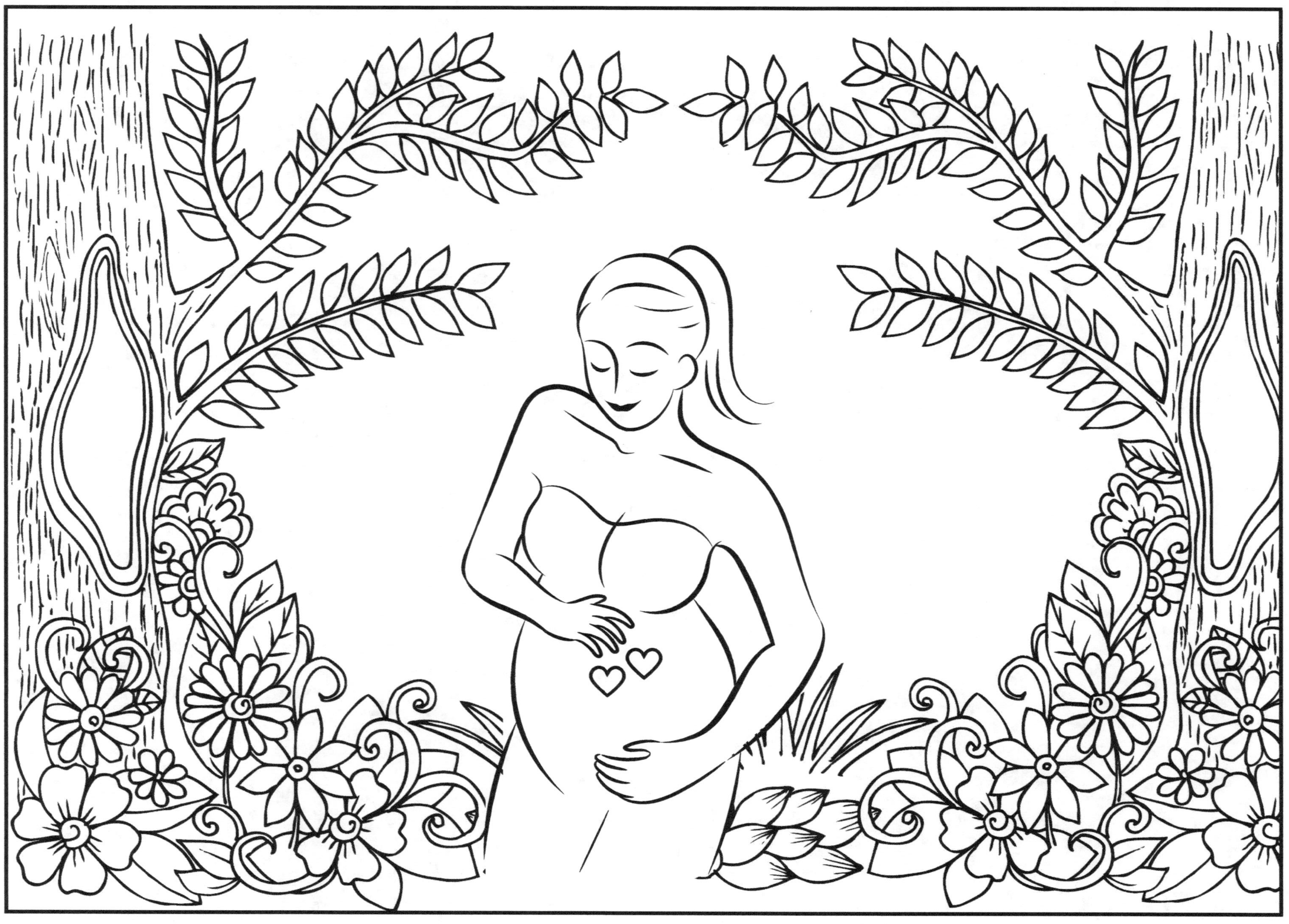

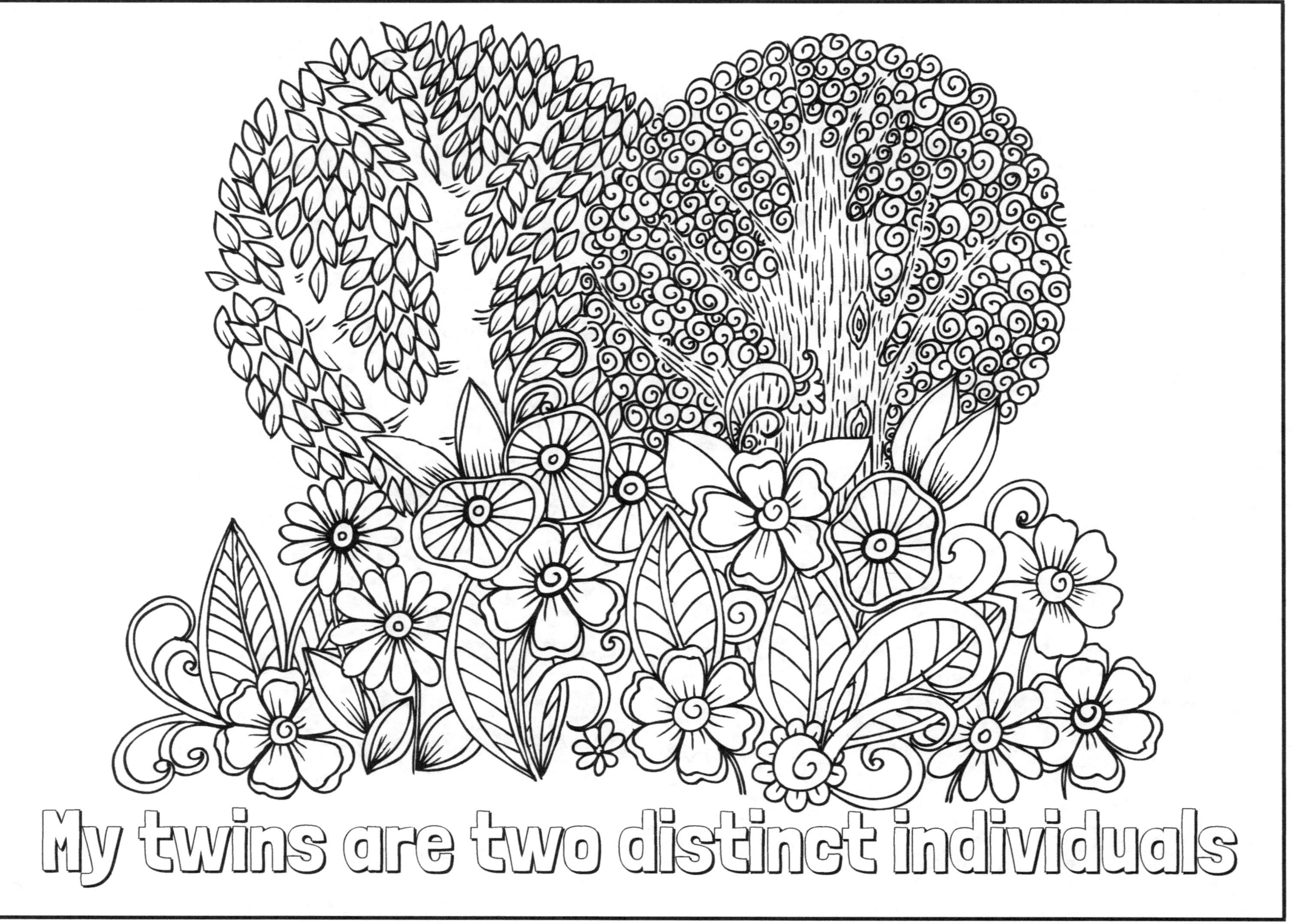
My twins are two distinct individuals

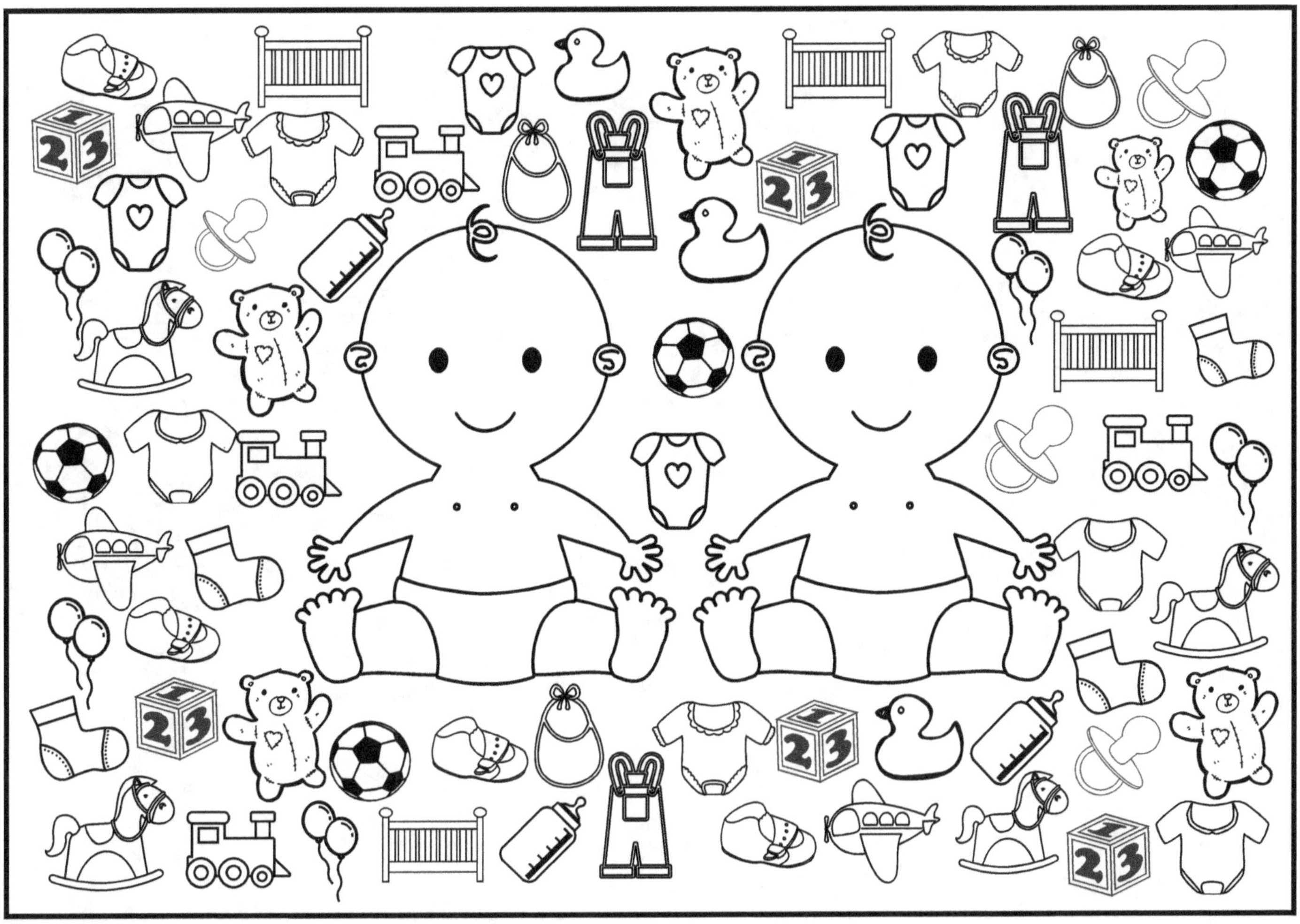

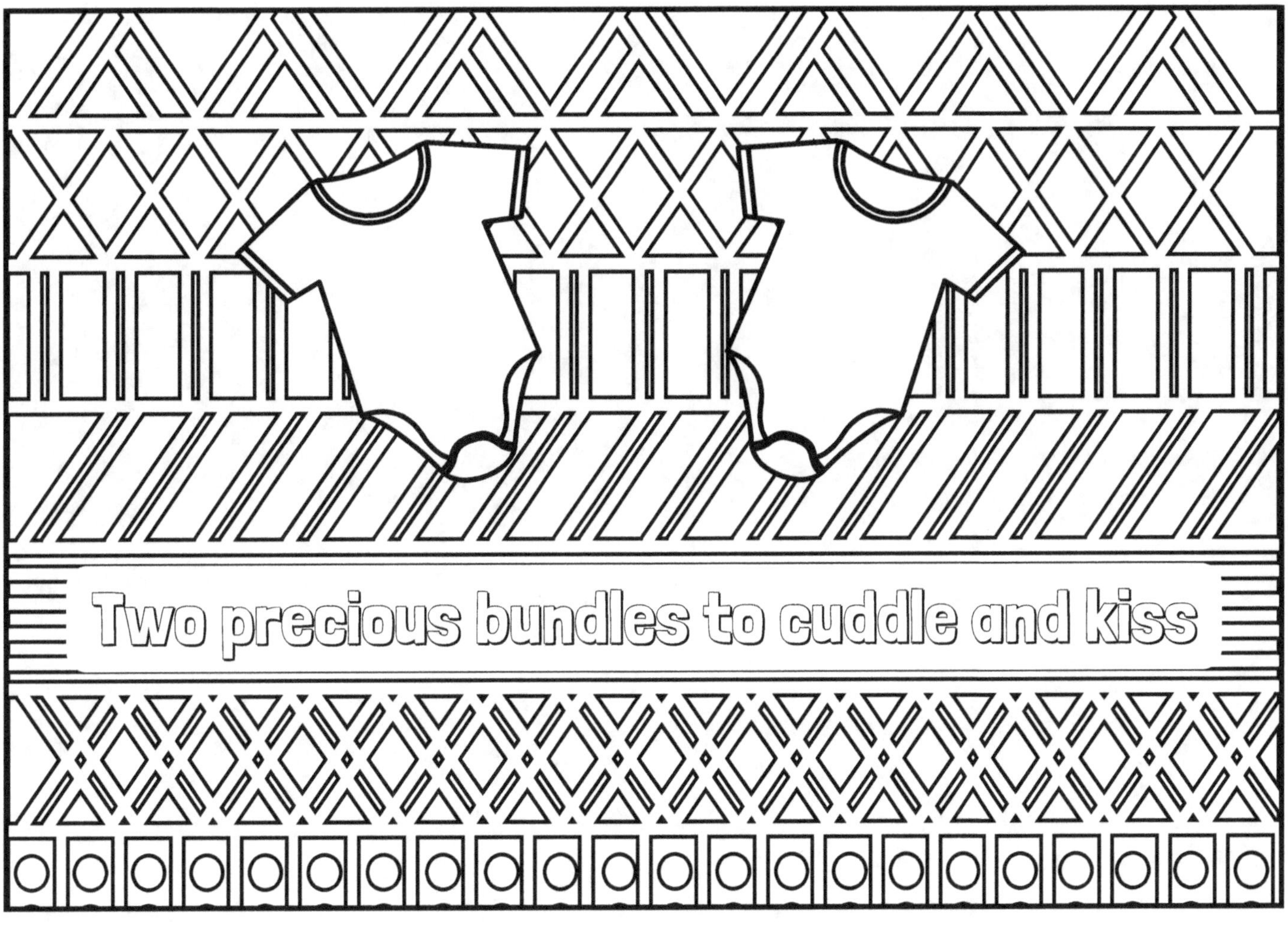

Two precious bundles to cuddle and kiss

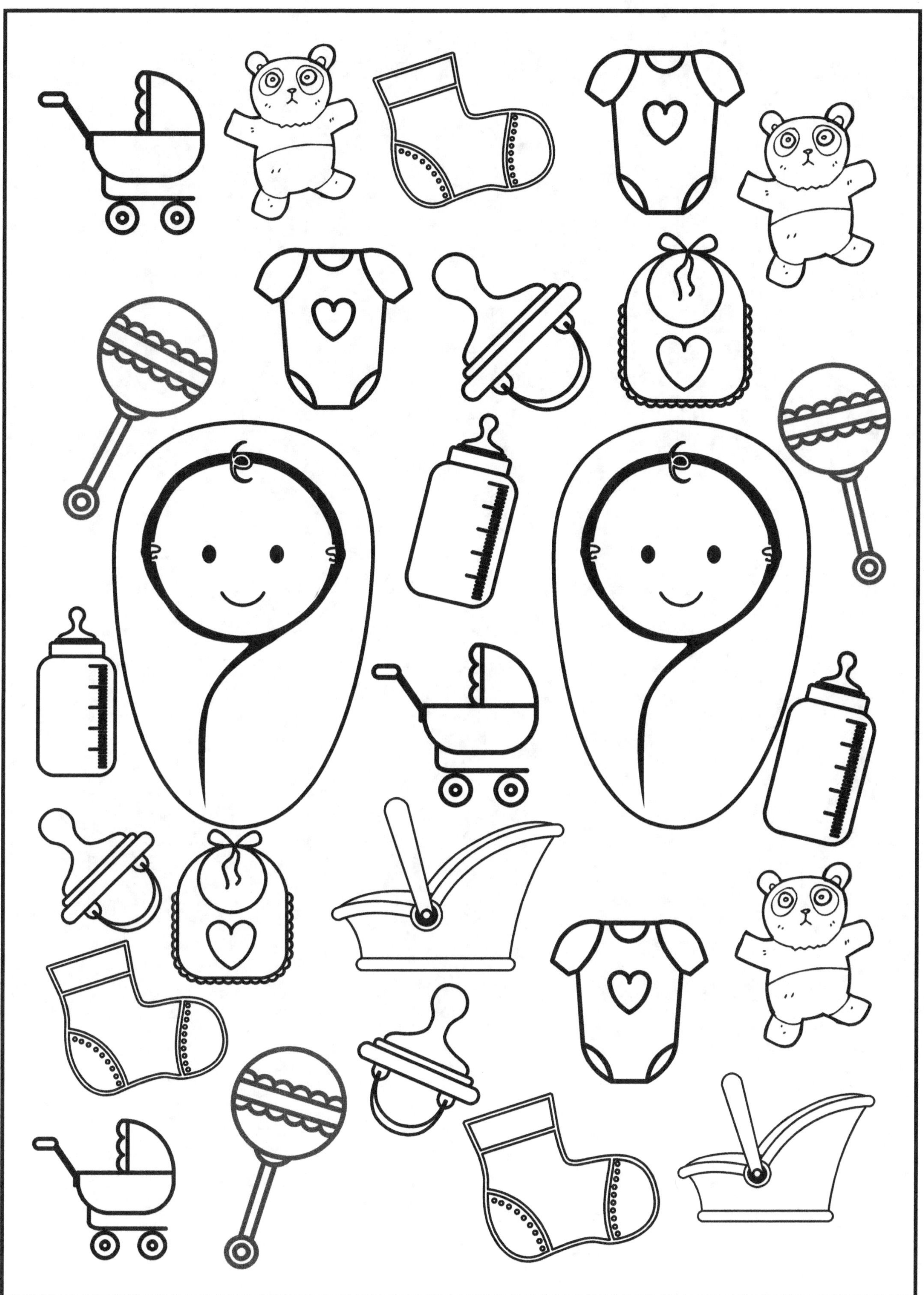

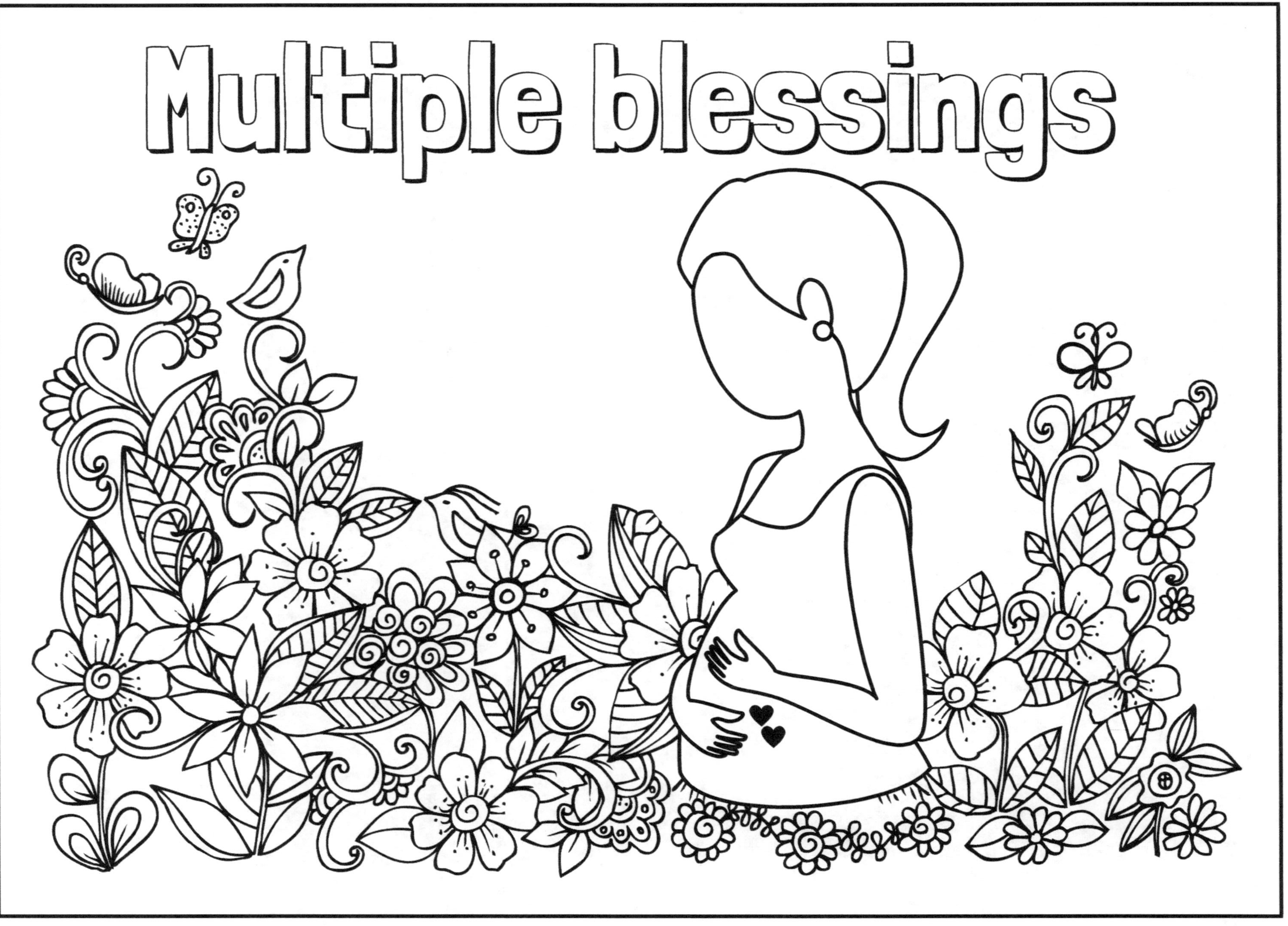

Multiple blessings

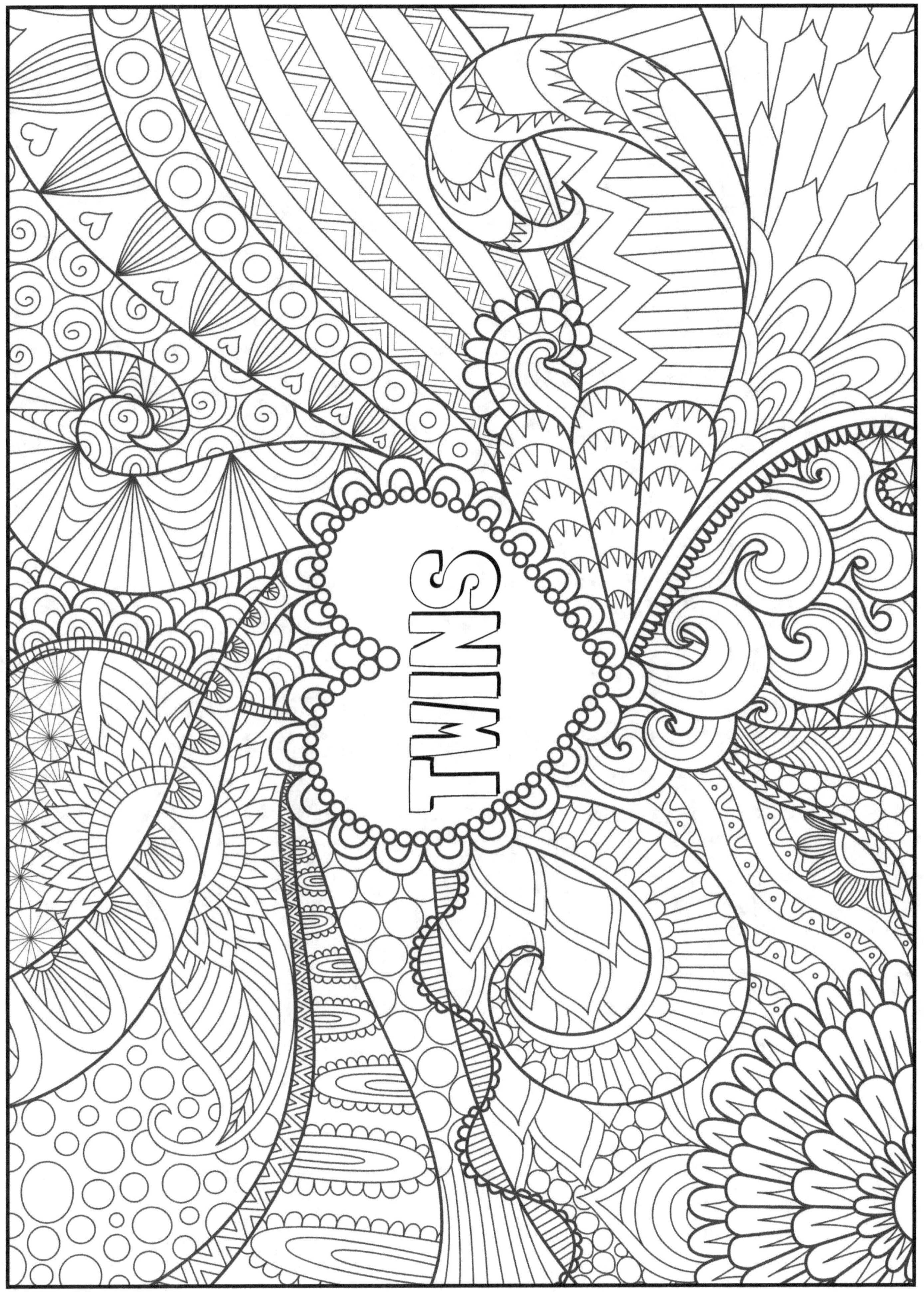

TWINS

Two to love

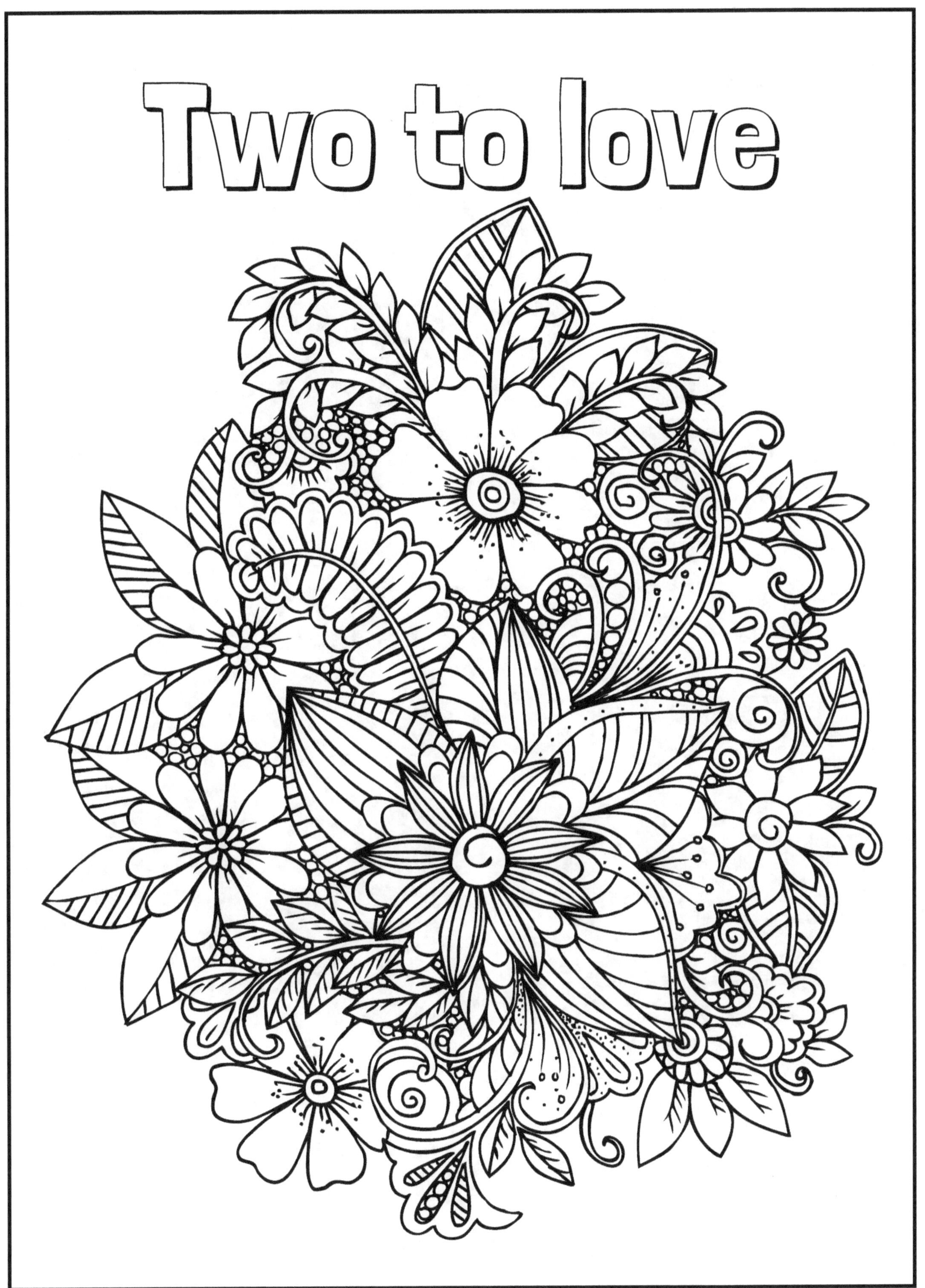

www.ingramcontent.com/pod-product-compliance
Lightning Source LLC
Chambersburg PA
CBHW080755030726
47592CB00009B/2874